ARTIFICIAL INTELLIGENCE (AI) AND ROBOTICS

FIRST EDITION

BY PRASUN BARUA

1

ABOUT

Welcome to Artificial intelligence (AI) and Robotics! This is a nonfiction science book which contains various topics on artificial intelligence (AI) and robotics. Artificial intelligence (AI) and robotics have revolutionized numerous industries and are reshaping the way we live and work. AI refers to the simulation of human intelligence in machines, allowing them to learn, reason, and make decisions. Robotics, on the other hand, involves the design and construction of physical machines that can interact with their environment. AI and robotics are intertwined fields, with AI providing the cognitive abilities for robots to perform complex tasks. Together, they have the potential to enhance productivity, efficiency, and innovation across various sectors. In manufacturing, robots equipped with AI can automate repetitive and dangerous tasks, leading to increased output and improved workplace safety. In healthcare, AI-powered robotic systems can assist in surgery, provide personalized patient care, and even perform tasks like medication delivery. Moreover, AI algorithms enable machines to analyze vast amounts of data and identify patterns, enabling advancements in fields like finance, transportation, and agriculture. AI-powered virtual assistants, chatbots, and recommendation systems have become integral parts of our daily lives, enhancing our digital experiences. However, the rapid advancement of AI and robotics also raises important ethical and societal considerations. Discussions on job displacement, privacy concerns, and the responsible use of AI are crucial to ensure a balanced and inclusive future. Artificial intelligence and robotics are driving transformative changes across industries, improving efficiency, and enabling new capabilities. Their potential for growth and innovation is vast, but their responsible and ethical implementation is paramount to harness their benefits for society as a whole. This is the first edition of the book. Thanks for reading the book.

TABLE OF CONTENTS

CHAPTER-1: WHAT IS ARTIFICIAL INTELLIGENCE (AI)?

Artificial Intelligence (AI) is a revolutionary field of computer science that focuses on developing intelligent machines capable of performing tasks that traditionally require human intelligence. It encompasses a wide range of techniques and approaches, including machine learning, natural language processing, computer vision, robotics, and expert systems. AI systems aim to emulate human cognitive abilities such as learning, reasoning, problem-solving, perception, and decision-making, opening up new possibilities across various industries and domains. In this essay, we will delve into the concept of AI, its historical development, key components and techniques, its impact on society, and future prospects.

The origins of AI can be traced back to the 1950s when computer scientists began envisioning machines that could simulate human intelligence. The Dartmouth Conference in 1956 is often considered the birthplace of AI as it brought together prominent researchers to discuss the possibilities of creating "thinking machines." Early AI research focused on symbolic approaches, using logical rules to represent knowledge and perform reasoning tasks. Notable early AI projects included the Logic Theorist, General Problem Solver, and the development of expert systems.

AI encompasses various components and techniques that enable machines to exhibit intelligent behavior.

a) Machine Learning: Machine learning is a subset of AI that involves the development of algorithms and models that allow machines to learn from data without explicit programming. It utilizes techniques such as supervised learning, unsupervised learning, and reinforcement learning to enable machines to recognize patterns, make predictions, and adapt to changing environments.

b) Natural Language Processing (NLP): NLP focuses on enabling machines to understand, interpret, and generate human language. It involves techniques such as text analysis, sentiment analysis, language translation, and speech recognition, facilitating human-machine communication.

c) Computer Vision: Computer vision enables machines to perceive and understand visual information. It involves techniques like image recognition, object detection, and video analysis, enabling machines to "see" and interpret visual data.

d) Robotics: Robotics combines AI with mechanical engineering to create intelligent machines that can interact with the physical world. Robotic systems incorporate perception, decision-making, and control to perform tasks autonomously or in collaboration with humans.

e) Expert Systems: Expert systems utilize knowledge engineering techniques to capture human expertise and provide intelligent advice or make decisions in specific domains. They rely on rule-based reasoning, inference engines, and knowledge representation to solve complex problems.

III. Impact of Artificial Intelligence on Society (600 words)

AI has already begun to reshape society across various domains, including healthcare, transportation, finance, entertainment, and education. Its impact can be observed in the following areas:

a) Healthcare: AI is revolutionizing healthcare by aiding in disease diagnosis, drug discovery, personalized medicine, and predictive analytics. Machine learning algorithms can analyze medical images, detect anomalies, and assist doctors in making more accurate diagnoses.

b) Transportation: Self-driving cars powered by AI have the potential to transform transportation systems, reducing accidents, optimizing traffic flow, and improving energy efficiency. AI-based navigation systems also enhance route planning and logistics.

c) Finance: AI is being utilized in the finance sector for fraud detection, algorithmic trading, credit scoring, and customer service chatbots. It enables faster and more accurate data analysis, risk assessment, and decision-making.

d) Entertainment: AI technologies are revolutionizing the entertainment industry through personalized recommendations, content creation, virtual reality (VR), and augmented reality (AR) experiences. AI-powered chatbots and virtual assistants enhance user engagement and interaction.

e) Education: AI has the potential to transform education by providing personalized learning experiences, intelligent tutoring systems, and automated grading. It can analyze student data to identify learning gaps and tailor educational content accordingly.

IV. Future Prospects and Challenges (350 words) The future of AI holds immense potential and challenges. As AI continues to advance, it is expected to revolutionize industries further and bring about societal transformations. However, several challenges need to be addressed, including:

a) Ethical Considerations: The development and deployment of AI systems raise ethical questions regarding privacy, bias, accountability, and job displacement. Ensuring fairness, transparency, and responsible use of AI technologies is crucial.

b) Data Privacy and Security: AI relies heavily on data, raising concerns about data privacy and security. Protecting sensitive information and preventing misuse or unauthorized access to data is a pressing challenge.

c) Human-AI Collaboration: As AI becomes more capable, establishing effective collaboration between humans and machines will be essential. Ensuring that AI systems augment human capabilities rather than replace them is crucial for a harmonious integration.

d) Robustness and Trustworthiness: AI systems must be robust, reliable, and trustworthy to gain widespread acceptance. Addressing issues such as adversarial attacks, system failures, and biased decision-making is crucial for building trust in AI technologies.

Artificial Intelligence has evolved significantly over the years, enabling machines to perform tasks that were once considered exclusive to human intelligence. Its impact on society is already visible, and the future prospects are both exciting and challenging. To harness the full potential of AI, it is essential to address ethical considerations, ensure data privacy and security, foster human-AI collaboration, and develop robust and trustworthy AI systems. By navigating these challenges effectively, we can unlock the transformative power of AI and shape a future where intelligent machines coexist harmoniously with humanity.

CHAPTER-2: CLASSIFICATIONS OF ARTIFICIAL INTELLIGENCE (AI)

Artificial Intelligence (AI) can be classified into different categories based on their capabilities and functionalities. Here are some common classifications of AI:

Narrow AI: Narrow AI, also known as weak AI, refers to AI systems that are designed to perform specific tasks or solve particular problems. These systems are focused on a narrow domain and excel in their specific area of expertise. Examples include voice assistants, recommendation algorithms, fraud detection systems, and autonomous vehicles.

General AI: General AI, also called strong AI or artificial general intelligence, represents AI systems that possess the ability to understand, learn, and apply knowledge across various domains, similar to human intelligence. These systems would be capable of performing any intellectual task that a human can do. Achieving true general AI remains a significant ongoing research challenge.

Machine Learning: Machine Learning (ML) is a subset of AI that focuses on algorithms and models that enable machines to learn from data and make predictions or decisions without being explicitly programmed. ML techniques include supervised learning, unsupervised learning, and reinforcement learning. ML is widely used in various applications, such as image recognition, natural language processing, and recommendation systems.

Deep Learning: Deep Learning is a subfield of machine learning that involves artificial neural networks with multiple layers (deep neural networks). These networks can automatically learn hierarchical representations of data, enabling them to process complex patterns and make accurate predictions. Deep learning has achieved remarkable success in areas such as image and speech recognition.

Natural Language Processing (NLP): Natural Language Processing focuses on enabling computers to understand, interpret, and generate human language. NLP techniques allow machines to process and analyze textual data, perform language translation, sentiment analysis, chatbot interactions, and more.

Computer Vision: Computer Vision involves the development of AI systems that can perceive and understand visual information from images or videos. It includes tasks like image recognition, object detection, facial recognition, and image generation.

Robotics: Robotics combines AI with physical machines to create intelligent systems that can interact with the physical world. Robotic AI involves perception, planning, control, and decision-making capabilities to enable robots to perform tasks autonomously or collaborate with humans in various settings.

These classifications represent different aspects and approaches within the field of AI, and many AI systems incorporate elements from multiple categories to achieve specific goals.

CHAPTER-3: HOW DOES ARTIFICIAL INTELLIGENCE (AI) WORK?

Artificial Intelligence (AI) systems work by utilizing various algorithms and techniques to process data, learn from it, make decisions or predictions, and perform tasks. Here's a general overview of how AI works:

Data Collection: AI systems require data to learn and make informed decisions. This data can be collected from various sources, such as sensors, databases, the internet, or user interactions.

Data Preprocessing: Once the data is collected, it often needs to be preprocessed to ensure its quality and compatibility with the AI algorithms. This step involves cleaning the data, handling missing values, normalizing or scaling the data, and transforming it into a suitable format for further analysis.

Algorithms and Models: AI systems employ different algorithms and models depending on the task at hand. For example, in machine learning, algorithms like decision trees, support vector machines, or neural networks are used. These algorithms learn from the provided data to recognize patterns, extract features, or make predictions.

Training the Model: In the training phase, the AI system is presented with labeled or unlabeled data and is guided to learn from it. In supervised learning, the AI system is provided with input-output pairs to learn the mapping between them. In unsupervised learning, the system identifies patterns or structures within the data. Reinforcement learning involves training the AI system through interaction with an environment and receiving feedback in the form of rewards or penalties.

Model Evaluation and Tuning: After the initial training, the AI model is evaluated using validation data to assess its performance and identify any shortcomings. If necessary, the model is fine-tuned by adjusting hyperparameters or modifying the architecture to improve its accuracy or efficiency.

Deployment and Inference: Once the AI model is trained and validated, it can be deployed to perform real-world tasks. During inference, the model takes new input data, processes it, and generates the desired outputs or predictions. This can involve tasks such as image recognition, natural language understanding, decision-making, or control of physical systems.

Continuous Learning and Improvement: AI systems can be designed to continuously learn and improve over time. They can be updated with new data to adapt to changing circumstances, improve accuracy, or handle new situations. This iterative process allows AI systems to refine their performance and stay up to date.

It's important to note that the specific implementation and techniques used in AI can vary based on the problem domain, the available data, and the desired outcomes. Different subfields of AI, such as machine learning, natural language processing, or computer vision, employ specific algorithms and methodologies tailored to their respective tasks.

CHAPTER-4: APPLICATIONS OF AI

Artificial Intelligence (AI) has a wide range of applications across various industries and domains. Here are some notable applications of AI:

Healthcare: AI is used for medical image analysis, disease diagnosis, drug discovery, personalized medicine, virtual nursing assistants, patient monitoring, and prediction of disease outbreaks.

Finance: AI is employed for fraud detection, algorithmic trading, credit scoring, risk assessment, customer service chatbots, financial planning, and robo-advisors for investment management.

Retail: AI powers recommender systems, demand forecasting, inventory management, personalized marketing, chatbots for customer support, and cashier-less stores.

Manufacturing and Robotics: AI is utilized for process automation, quality control, predictive maintenance, supply chain optimization, collaborative robots (cobots), and autonomous vehicles in industrial settings.

Transportation: AI plays a crucial role in autonomous vehicles, traffic prediction, route optimization, fleet management, smart transportation systems, and driver assistance systems.

Customer Service: AI-driven chatbots and virtual assistants are used for customer support, natural language understanding, sentiment analysis, and personalized interactions.

Natural Language Processing: AI enables language translation, sentiment analysis, chatbots, voice assistants, voice recognition, text summarization, and language generation.

Education: AI is employed in intelligent tutoring systems, personalized learning platforms, automated grading, plagiarism detection, and adaptive learning environments.

Cybersecurity: AI helps in threat detection, anomaly detection, malware detection, behavioral biometrics, fraud prevention, and network security.

Entertainment and Gaming: AI powers virtual reality (VR) and augmented reality (AR) experiences, game playing agents, content recommendation, and personalized entertainment platforms.

Agriculture: AI is utilized for crop monitoring, yield prediction, pest detection, irrigation optimization, livestock management, and autonomous farming.

Energy: AI enables energy demand prediction, energy grid optimization, predictive maintenance of equipment, and renewable energy management.

These are just a few examples, and AI is being applied in numerous other domains, including law, marketing, environmental conservation, social sciences, and more. The potential applications of AI continue to expand as technology advances and new opportunities arise.

CHAPTER-5: PROCESSING OF AN AI ALGORITHM

The processing of an AI algorithm involves several steps, from data preparation to model training and inference. Here's a general overview of the AI algorithm processing pipeline:

Data Collection: The first step is to collect relevant data for the AI algorithm. This data can be obtained from various sources, such as databases, files, APIs, or sensors. The data should be representative and cover the aspects necessary for the specific AI task.

Data Preprocessing: Once the data is collected, it often requires preprocessing to ensure its quality and compatibility with the AI algorithm. This step involves tasks like cleaning the data (removing noise, handling missing values), transforming the data into a suitable format (numeric encoding, one-hot encoding), and splitting the data into training, validation, and testing sets.

Feature Extraction: In many AI tasks, the raw data needs to be transformed into a feature representation that the algorithm can effectively learn from. Feature extraction involves selecting or engineering relevant features that capture the characteristics or patterns in the data. This step can include techniques like dimensionality reduction, feature scaling, or applying domain-specific knowledge.

Algorithm Selection: Based on the nature of the problem and the characteristics of the data, an appropriate AI algorithm is chosen. The algorithm selection depends on the task, such as classification, regression, clustering, or sequence generation. Common AI algorithms include decision trees, support vector machines, neural networks, random forests, or gradient boosting algorithms.

Model Training: The selected algorithm is trained using the prepared data. During the training process, the algorithm learns from the input data to make accurate predictions or decisions. The algorithm adjusts its internal parameters iteratively by minimizing a loss function that quantifies the difference between the predicted outputs and the true labels (in supervised learning) or the data structure (in unsupervised learning).

Model Evaluation: After the model is trained, it needs to be evaluated to assess its performance. The evaluation is typically done using a separate validation dataset or through cross-validation techniques. Common evaluation metrics depend on the specific task, such as accuracy, precision, recall, F1 score, mean squared error, or area under the ROC curve.

Hyperparameter Tuning: AI algorithms often have hyperparameters that control the behavior of the model. Hyperparameters include the learning rate, regularization strength, network architecture, or the number of trees in an ensemble. These hyperparameters can significantly affect the model's performance. Techniques like grid search, random search, or Bayesian optimization can be used to find the optimal hyperparameter settings.

Model Deployment and Inference: Once the model is trained and fine-tuned, it can be deployed to perform real-world tasks. During the inference phase, the model takes new, unseen data as input and generates predictions or decisions. The processed data is passed through the trained model, and the output is produced based on the learned patterns and relationships.

It's important to note that the specific details of AI algorithm processing can vary depending on the algorithm, the problem domain, and the available data. Different algorithms have different training and inference procedures, and some may require specialized techniques or additional steps to improve performance or handle specific challenges.

CHAPTER-6: DEVELOPING AI FOR VARIOUS APPLICATIONS

Developing AI for various applications involves several key steps. Here is a general roadmap to guide you through the process:

Define the Problem: Clearly articulate the problem you want to solve or the task you want the AI system to perform. Understand the requirements, constraints, and objectives of the application. This step helps in setting the direction for AI development.

Gather and Prepare Data: Collect relevant data that is representative of the problem domain. This data will be used for training and evaluating the AI model. Clean the data, handle missing values, remove outliers, and preprocess it into a suitable format for further analysis.

Select AI Techniques: Based on the problem definition and data characteristics, choose the appropriate AI techniques and algorithms. Consider options like machine learning (supervised, unsupervised, or reinforcement learning), natural language processing, computer vision, or other specialized techniques.

Design the AI Model: Define the architecture and structure of the AI model. This includes selecting the appropriate type of neural network, defining the number of layers, choosing activation functions, and designing the model's flow. Depending on the complexity of the problem, you may need to explore pre-trained models or create a custom model architecture.

Train the Model: Use the prepared data to train the AI model. Split the data into training and validation sets. Apply the selected algorithm to learn patterns and make predictions. Tune hyperparameters, optimize the model, and iterate on the training process until the desired performance is achieved. Validate the model using the validation set to ensure it generalizes well.

Evaluate and Refine: Assess the performance of the trained model using appropriate evaluation metrics. Identify areas where the model may be lacking or underperforming. Fine-tune the model, adjust hyperparameters, or revisit the data preprocessing steps if necessary. Repeat this cycle until the model meets the desired performance benchmarks.

Deployment and Integration: Once the model is trained and evaluated, it needs to be deployed into a production environment. Integrate the AI model into the application or system where it will be used. Ensure the necessary infrastructure, software, and dependencies are in place for the model to operate effectively. Test the deployment thoroughly to ensure it functions as expected.

Monitor and Update: Continuously monitor the AI system's performance in the real-world environment. Collect feedback, measure its accuracy, and identify areas for improvement. Update the model periodically to incorporate new data, adapt to changing patterns, or address emerging challenges. Maintenance and regular updates are crucial for maintaining optimal performance.

Ethical Considerations: Consider the ethical implications of your AI system. Address issues related to data privacy, bias, transparency, fairness, and accountability. Ensure that your AI system adheres to legal and ethical standards.

Remember that developing AI for different applications can vary in complexity and may require domain-specific knowledge or expertise. It's crucial to stay updated with the latest advancements in AI research and leverage existing libraries, frameworks, and tools that facilitate AI development. Collaboration and interdisciplinary approaches can also enhance the development process by incorporating diverse perspectives and skills.

CHAPTER-7: MATHEMATICAL AND LOGICAL PRINCIPLES OF AI

Artificial Intelligence (AI) relies on various mathematical and logical principles. Here are some fundamental concepts and techniques used in AI:

Probability and Statistics: Probability theory is used in AI to model uncertainty and make decisions in uncertain environments. Statistical methods are employed for data analysis, hypothesis testing, and parameter estimation. Probabilistic models like Bayesian networks and Markov models are used for reasoning and decision-making.

Linear Algebra: Linear algebra is used extensively in AI, especially in machine learning and deep learning. Matrix operations, vector spaces, eigenvalues, and eigenvectors are fundamental concepts used in representing and manipulating data, as well as in linear transformations and optimization algorithms.

Calculus: Calculus plays a crucial role in optimization algorithms used in AI. Techniques like gradient descent, which involve computing derivatives and finding local minima or maxima, are used to train models and adjust parameters.

Logic and Predicate Calculus: Logic forms the foundation of reasoning and knowledge representation in AI. Propositional logic and predicate calculus are used to represent and manipulate knowledge, perform reasoning, and infer new conclusions.

Graph Theory: Graph theory is used to model relationships and dependencies between entities in AI. Graph-based algorithms like breadth-first search, depth-first search, and graph traversal are employed in tasks like pathfinding, recommendation systems, and social network analysis.

Information Theory: Information theory is used to quantify and analyze the amount of information in data. Concepts like entropy, mutual information, and compression algorithms are utilized in tasks like feature selection, data encoding, and model evaluation.

Optimization: Optimization algorithms, such as gradient descent, genetic algorithms, and simulated annealing, are employed in AI to optimize model parameters, solve constraint satisfaction problems, and find optimal solutions in search spaces.

Set Theory: Set theory is used to represent and manipulate collections of objects or entities. Concepts like union, intersection, and complement are applied in tasks like pattern recognition, clustering, and rule-based systems.

Neural Networks: Neural networks, a key component of AI, are mathematical models inspired by the structure and functioning of biological neural networks. These networks consist of interconnected nodes (neurons) and use mathematical operations like weighted sums and activation functions to process and learn from data.

Decision Theory: Decision theory is used to make rational decisions in AI. It involves utility theory, decision trees, and game theory to model decision-making under uncertainty, strategic interactions, and optimization of outcomes.

These are some of the mathematical and logical foundations used in AI. However, it's important to note that AI is a vast field with various subfields, and specific techniques and algorithms within AI may require additional mathematical and logical principles tailored to their respective domains.

CHAPTER-8: DEVELOPING AI FOR VARIOUS SOCIAL MEDIA

Developing AI for various social media applications involves a combination of data collection, preprocessing, algorithm selection, and model training. Here's a high-level overview of the steps involved:

Define the Objective: Determine the specific objective or task you want to achieve with AI in the context of social media. It could be content recommendation, sentiment analysis, user profiling, spam detection, or social network analysis, among others.

Data Collection: Gather relevant data from social media platforms. This data may include user profiles, posts, comments, likes, shares, and other interactions. APIs provided by social media platforms can be used to access and collect data in a structured manner.

Data Preprocessing: Clean and preprocess the collected data to ensure its quality and compatibility with AI algorithms. This step involves removing noise, handling missing values, normalizing or scaling the data, and transforming it into a suitable format for analysis.

Feature Extraction: Extract meaningful features from the data that capture the relevant information for the chosen social media application. This can involve techniques like natural language processing (NLP) for text analysis, image or video processing for multimedia content, or network analysis for social connections.

Algorithm Selection: Choose the appropriate AI algorithms based on the specific task. For example, for content recommendation, you might use collaborative filtering or content-based filtering algorithms. For sentiment analysis, you might use machine learning algorithms like support vector machines or deep learning models like recurrent neural networks.

Model Training: Train the selected AI model using the preprocessed data. This typically involves feeding the labeled data (if available) into the model and adjusting its parameters iteratively to learn patterns and make accurate predictions. If labeled data is not available, unsupervised learning or semi-supervised learning techniques can be employed.

Model Evaluation: Evaluate the trained model using appropriate metrics and evaluation techniques. This helps assess the model's performance and determine its effectiveness in achieving the defined objective. Cross-validation or holdout validation can be used to estimate the model's generalization performance.

Deployment and Integration: Integrate the trained AI model into the social media platform or application where it will be utilized. This could involve implementing APIs, developing user interfaces, or integrating the model into existing systems. Ensure the necessary infrastructure, scalability, and real-time processing capabilities are in place.

Continuous Learning and Improvement: Monitor the AI system's performance in real-world usage and collect feedback from users. Incorporate user feedback and new data to continuously improve the model's accuracy, relevance, and responsiveness. This can involve periodic retraining of the model or online learning techniques.

Ethical Considerations: Consider ethical aspects, such as user privacy, fairness, and transparency, when developing AI for social media. Ensure compliance with relevant privacy regulations and address potential biases that may arise from the data or algorithms used.

It's important to note that developing AI for social media applications requires a deep understanding of the specific social media platforms, their APIs, and the unique characteristics of social media data. Collaboration with domain experts, social media platform providers, and data scientists can greatly enhance the development process.

CHAPTER-9: BENEFITS OF AI

Artificial Intelligence (AI) offers a wide range of benefits and transformative potential across various fields. Here are some key benefits of AI:

Automation and Efficiency: AI enables automation of tasks that were previously performed by humans, leading to increased efficiency and productivity. AI algorithms can handle repetitive and mundane tasks, freeing up human resources to focus on more complex and strategic activities.

Improved Accuracy and Precision: AI algorithms can process large volumes of data quickly and accurately, leading to improved decision-making and reduced errors. AI-powered systems can analyze complex datasets, detect patterns, and make predictions with higher precision than traditional methods.

Enhanced Personalization: AI enables personalized experiences by analyzing vast amounts of user data and tailoring recommendations, services, and products to individual preferences. This is particularly valuable in areas like e-commerce, marketing, and content delivery, where personalization can improve customer satisfaction and engagement.

Advanced Data Analysis and Insights: AI algorithms can extract insights, trends, and patterns from large and complex datasets, enabling organizations to make data-driven decisions. AI-powered analytics tools can uncover valuable information that may not be apparent through traditional analysis methods, leading to better business intelligence and strategic planning.

Automation of Dangerous and Tedious Tasks: AI can be deployed in environments that are hazardous or challenging for humans, such as exploring deep-sea environments, handling toxic substances, or conducting space exploration. By automating such tasks, AI can minimize risks to human life and enhance safety.

Rapid and Continuous Learning: AI systems can learn from data and experience, continually improving their performance over time. Machine learning algorithms can adapt and optimize their models based on feedback, leading to more accurate predictions and better performance in various applications.

Assistive Technologies: AI-powered assistive technologies can aid individuals with disabilities or special needs. Speech recognition, natural language processing, and computer vision algorithms can enable communication, accessibility, and independent living for people with physical or cognitive impairments.

Medical Diagnosis and Healthcare: AI has the potential to revolutionize healthcare by aiding in medical diagnosis, image analysis, and treatment planning. AI algorithms can analyze medical images, interpret clinical data, and assist in early detection of diseases, leading to more accurate diagnoses and improved patient outcomes.

Innovation and Research: AI fuels innovation by pushing the boundaries of what is possible. AI research drives advancements in areas like machine learning, natural language processing, computer vision, and robotics, opening up new possibilities for solving complex problems and creating novel applications.

It's important to note that the ethical considerations surrounding AI, such as transparency, fairness, privacy, and accountability, need to be carefully addressed to ensure responsible and beneficial deployment of AI technologies.

CHAPTER-10: WHAT IS ROBOTICS?

Robotics is a branch of technology and engineering that deals with the design, construction, operation, and programming of robots. A robot is a mechanical device or an artificial agent capable of autonomously or semi-autonomously performing tasks and interacting with its environment.

Robots are designed to carry out a wide range of functions, often with the goal of automating tasks that are repetitive, dangerous, or impractical for humans to perform. They can be found in various domains, including manufacturing, healthcare, agriculture, exploration, transportation, and entertainment.

Robotics involves several key components:

1. Mechanical Structure: The physical design and structure of a robot, including its body, limbs, sensors, actuators, and mechanisms. The mechanical structure determines the robot's physical capabilities and how it interacts with its environment.

2. Sensors: Robots use various sensors to perceive and gather information about their surroundings. Common sensors include cameras, lasers, proximity sensors, tactile sensors, and inertial

measurement units (IMUs). These sensors provide input to the robot's control system.

3. Control System: The control system of a robot is responsible for processing sensory information, making decisions, and generating appropriate commands for the actuators. It can range from simple rule-based systems to sophisticated algorithms based on artificial intelligence and machine learning techniques.

4. Actuators: Actuators are the components responsible for moving and manipulating the robot's body and limbs. Examples of actuators include motors, hydraulic or pneumatic systems, and artificial muscles. They translate commands from the control system into physical movements.

5. Programming and Algorithms: Robotics involves developing software and algorithms to control the robot's behavior and enable it to perform specific tasks. Programming languages like C++, Python, and MATLAB are commonly used, along with specialized robot programming frameworks and libraries.

6. Human-Robot Interaction: As robots become more advanced and integrated into human environments, human-robot interaction (HRI)

becomes increasingly important. HRI focuses on designing interfaces and communication methods to enable effective collaboration and communication between humans and robots.

Robotics is a multidisciplinary field that draws from various domains, including mechanical engineering, electrical engineering, computer science, artificial intelligence, control systems, and cognitive science. It encompasses both hardware and software aspects, with the goal of creating intelligent and capable machines that can perform tasks autonomously or with minimal human intervention.

CHAPTER-11: TYPES OF ROBOTICS

There are several types of robotics based on their application areas and characteristics. Here are some common types of robotics:

1. Industrial Robotics: Industrial robots are used in manufacturing and production environments. They are typically designed for tasks such as assembly, welding, painting, material handling, and quality control. Industrial robots are often large, powerful, and programmed to perform repetitive tasks with high precision and speed.

2. Service Robotics: Service robots are intended to assist and interact with humans in various settings. They are designed to perform tasks in domains like healthcare, hospitality, retail, education, and domestic chores. Examples include robot assistants in hospitals, robotic vacuum cleaners, and personal assistance robots for the elderly.

3. Medical Robotics: Medical robots are used in healthcare for a range of purposes, including surgery, rehabilitation, diagnostics, and patient care. Surgical robots, for instance, assist surgeons

during procedures, enabling precise movements and enhancing minimally invasive surgery. Robotic prosthetics and exoskeletons aid in rehabilitation and mobility support.

4. Autonomous Vehicles: Autonomous vehicles, such as self-driving cars, trucks, and drones, fall under the realm of robotics. These vehicles leverage a combination of sensors, AI algorithms, and control systems to navigate and operate without human intervention. They have the potential to revolutionize transportation and logistics.

5. Space Robotics: Space robots are designed for exploration and operations in outer space. They assist in tasks like satellite deployment and maintenance, planetary exploration, and extraterrestrial research. Examples include rovers like NASA's Mars rovers and robotic arms on spacecraft.

6. Aerial and Underwater Robotics: Aerial robots, commonly known as drones, are used for various purposes, including aerial photography, surveillance, mapping, and delivery services. Underwater robots, also known as remotely operated vehicles (ROVs), are employed for tasks

such as underwater exploration, marine research, and offshore operations.

7. Humanoid Robotics: Humanoid robots are designed to resemble humans in appearance and behavior. They aim to mimic human movements and interact with humans in a more intuitive and natural way. Humanoid robots are used in areas such as research, entertainment, education, and social interaction experiments.

8. Military and Defense Robotics: Military robots are employed for reconnaissance, bomb disposal, surveillance, and other tasks that are hazardous or inaccessible to humans. These robots can operate on land, air, or water, and they assist in enhancing situational awareness and protecting personnel.

These are just a few examples of the different types of robotics. The field of robotics is continually evolving, and new types of robots with specialized capabilities are being developed for various applications and industries.

CHAPTER-12: HOW ROBOTICS WORKS?

Robotics involves a combination of hardware and software components working together to enable the functioning of a robot. Here is an overview of how robotics works:

1. Perception: Robots perceive and gather information about their environment using various sensors such as cameras, lasers, proximity sensors, and microphones. These sensors capture data related to the robot's surroundings, including objects, obstacles, sounds, and other relevant information.

2. Processing and Control: The sensor data is processed by the robot's control system, which can consist of a combination of hardware and software components. The control system analyzes the sensor data, makes decisions, and generates commands for the robot's actuators.

3. Decision Making: Based on the processed sensor data, the control system applies algorithms and decision-making techniques to determine the appropriate actions for the robot to take. This can involve simple rule-based systems, algorithms

based on artificial intelligence and machine learning, or a combination of both.

4. Actuation: The control system generates commands that are sent to the robot's actuators. Actuators are the components responsible for moving and manipulating the robot's body and limbs. They can be motors, hydraulic or pneumatic systems, or other mechanisms that translate the control commands into physical movements.

5. Feedback and Iteration: As the robot performs actions, it receives feedback from its sensors, allowing it to monitor the results of its actions and make adjustments if needed. This feedback loop enables the robot to adapt and respond to changes in its environment or to correct errors in its actions.

6. Human-Robot Interaction (HRI): In many cases, robots interact with humans. HRI focuses on designing interfaces and communication methods to facilitate effective collaboration and communication between humans and robots. This can involve voice commands, gestures, touchscreens, or other forms of interaction.

7. Learning and Adaptation: Some robots have the ability to learn from their experiences and improve their performance over time. Machine learning

techniques, such as reinforcement learning, can be employed to enable robots to learn from feedback and adjust their behavior accordingly.

It's important to note that the specific workings of a robot can vary depending on its type, purpose, and complexity. Different types of robots may employ different sensors, actuators, control systems, and algorithms tailored to their specific tasks and environments. Robotics is a multidisciplinary field that combines knowledge from areas such as mechanical engineering, electrical engineering, computer science, artificial intelligence, and control systems to develop intelligent and capable machines.

how robots are built?

Robots are typically built through a combination of mechanical design, electronics, programming, and integration of various components. The process of making a robot involves several stages, which can vary depending on the complexity and purpose of the robot. Here is a general overview of how robots are made:

1. Conceptualization and Design:
   - Define the purpose and requirements of the robot.

- Determine the tasks the robot needs to perform and the environment it will operate in.
- Create a conceptual design that outlines the robot's overall structure, size, and capabilities.
- Develop detailed mechanical designs, specifying the robot's body, limbs, joints, and other physical components.

2. Mechanical Construction:
   - Fabricate the mechanical components of the robot, which may involve cutting, shaping, and assembling materials such as metal, plastic, or composites.
   - Build the robot's body, limbs, and joints according to the design specifications.
   - Integrate mechanical systems like motors, gears, and linkages to enable movement and manipulation.

3. Electrical and Electronic Integration:
   - Install and wire electronic components such as sensors, actuators, microcontrollers, and power systems.

- Connect sensors to appropriate interfaces and integrate them with the robot's control system.
- Install actuators and connect them to the control system to enable physical movement.

4. Software Development:
- Develop the software that controls the robot's behavior and functionality.
- Write code to interface with sensors, process sensor data, make decisions, and generate commands for the actuators.
- Program algorithms and logic for tasks such as navigation, object recognition, or grasping.

5. Integration and Testing:
- Assemble the mechanical and electronic components into the final robot.
- Integrate the software with the hardware and verify that all systems function properly.
- Conduct testing and debugging to ensure the robot operates as intended.

Iteratively refine and optimize the robot's design and software based on test results and feedback.

6. Deployment and Maintenance:

- Deploy the robot to its intended environment and perform any necessary calibrations or adjustments.
- Monitor the robot's performance, gather feedback, and make improvements as needed.
- Provide regular maintenance, including replacing worn-out parts, updating software, and addressing any issues that arise.

The process of making a robot involves expertise from various fields, including mechanical engineering, electrical engineering, computer science, and robotics. Collaboration between specialists in these areas is often required to create a functioning and effective robot. The complexity of the process can vary widely depending on the type and purpose of the robot being developed.

CHAPTER-13: APPLICATIONS OF ROBOTICS

Robotics has numerous applications across various industries and domains. Here are some common applications of robotics:

1. Manufacturing and Industrial Automation: Robotics plays a crucial role in manufacturing industries, where robots are used for tasks such as assembly, welding, painting, material handling, packaging, and quality control. Industrial automation improves productivity, efficiency, and precision in production processes.

2. Healthcare: Robots are employed in healthcare for a range of purposes. Surgical robots assist surgeons in performing minimally invasive procedures with enhanced precision and control. Robots are also used in rehabilitation to aid in physical therapy, gait training, and mobility assistance. Additionally, robots can support tasks such as medication delivery, patient monitoring, and elder care.

3. Agriculture: Robotics is being increasingly utilized in agriculture to improve efficiency and productivity. Robots can perform tasks like planting, harvesting, sorting, and spraying in fields or indoor farming environments. They can also monitor crop health, collect data, and aid in precision agriculture techniques.

4. Logistics and Warehousing: Robotics is transforming logistics and warehousing operations. Automated guided vehicles (AGVs) and robotic arms are employed for efficient and accurate movement, sorting, and stacking of goods in warehouses. Robots can also assist in order fulfillment, inventory management, and delivery processes.

5. Exploration and Space: Robots are extensively used in space exploration missions. Robotic rovers and landers are deployed to explore other planets and moons, collect samples, and conduct scientific experiments. Space robots assist in satellite servicing, repairs, and maintenance tasks.

6. Defense and Security: Robots are utilized for various defense and security applications. Unmanned aerial vehicles (UAVs) and drones provide aerial surveillance, reconnaissance, and

monitoring capabilities. Robots are also employed for bomb disposal, hazardous material handling, and search-and-rescue operations.

7. Education and Research: Robots are valuable tools for educational purposes and scientific research. They can be used to teach programming, robotics, and STEM concepts to students. Researchers employ robots to study human-robot interaction, artificial intelligence, machine learning, and cognitive robotics.

8. Entertainment and Hospitality: Robots are increasingly employed in the entertainment and hospitality industry. They can serve as interactive companions, guides, or performers in theme parks, museums, and exhibitions. Robots are also used in hotels and restaurants for tasks like room service, concierge services, and food preparation.

9. Environmental Monitoring and Cleanup: Robots are used for environmental monitoring and cleanup tasks. Underwater robots can explore and monitor marine environments, while drones and ground robots aid in land-based environmental surveys. Robots are also employed in cleaning operations for areas like oil spills or hazardous environments.

These are just a few examples of the applications of robotics. The field of robotics continues to evolve, and robots are being developed for a wide range of industries and domains to improve efficiency, safety, and productivity.

CHAPTER-14: HOW TO BUILD A ROBOT FOR MANUFACTURING INDUSTRY

Building a robot for the manufacturing industry involves several steps and considerations. Here is a detailed explanation of the process:

Define the Purpose and Scope:

Determine the specific task(s) you want the robot to perform. It could be assembly, material handling, welding, painting, inspection, or any other repetitive task in the manufacturing process.

Identify the specific requirements and constraints, such as payload capacity, speed, precision, workspace, and safety standards.

Conduct a Feasibility Study:

Evaluate the technical feasibility and economic viability of the robot project.

Consider factors like cost, return on investment (ROI), potential benefits, and risks.

Conceptual Design:

Based on the task requirements, decide on the robot's configuration (e.g., articulated arm, SCARA, cartesian, delta, etc.) and end-effector (gripper, tool, etc.).

Consider the workspace layout, reach, and mobility of the robot.

Select appropriate sensors (vision systems, proximity sensors, force/torque sensors, etc.) for perception and feedback.

Mechanical Design:

Develop a detailed mechanical design of the robot.

Choose suitable materials, components, and actuators based on the task requirements.

Ensure the robot's structural integrity, rigidity, and safety.

Consider ergonomics and ease of maintenance.

Electrical and Electronic Design:

Design the electrical and electronic systems of the robot.

Select appropriate motors, drives, and controllers based on the robot's mechanical design and performance requirements.

Design the power supply and wiring system.

Integrate safety features like emergency stop buttons, limit switches, and interlocks.

Software Development:

Develop the robot's control software, which includes motion control, path planning, and task execution.

Implement algorithms for perception, object recognition, and localization, if required.

Use programming languages and tools suitable for the robot's controller and interface.

Prototyping and Testing:

Build a prototype of the robot based on the designs.

Test the mechanical, electrical, and software systems individually and as an integrated system.

Verify that the robot meets the defined performance criteria, such as accuracy, repeatability, and cycle time.

Iterate on the design and make necessary adjustments based on test results.

Production and Deployment:

Once the prototype passes all tests, prepare for production.

Source the necessary components, materials, and subsystems in the required quantities.

Manufacture the robot according to the finalized design.

Conduct final quality checks before deployment.

Installation and Commissioning:

Install the robot in the manufacturing facility.

Integrate it with the existing infrastructure, such as conveyor systems or other machinery.

Calibrate the robot, including setting motion limits and end-effector parameters.

Test the robot's performance in the actual production environment.

Training and Maintenance:

Train the operators and maintenance personnel on how to use and maintain the robot safely and effectively.

Develop standard operating procedures (SOPs) and safety protocols.

Establish a maintenance schedule and conduct regular inspections, repairs, and software updates.

Throughout the entire process, it is important to involve experts in robotics, engineering, and manufacturing to ensure the robot meets the required standards and effectively fulfills its intended purpose in the manufacturing industry.

CHAPTER-15: BENEFITS OF ROBOTICS

Robotics offers a range of benefits across various industries and applications. Here are some key benefits of robotics:

Increased Efficiency and Productivity: Robots can perform tasks with speed, accuracy, and consistency, leading to improved efficiency and productivity in various domains. They can work non-stop, reducing the need for breaks or shifts, and perform repetitive tasks without experiencing fatigue or loss of concentration.

Enhanced Precision and Quality: Robots are capable of executing tasks with high precision and accuracy, reducing errors and increasing the quality of outputs. This is particularly valuable in manufacturing, where robots can consistently produce identical products and perform intricate assembly or welding operations with minimal variations.

Improved Workplace Safety: Robots can be employed to handle hazardous, repetitive, or physically demanding tasks, reducing the risk of workplace injuries and accidents. They can operate in dangerous environments such as nuclear facilities, mines, or disaster zones, where human presence might be risky.

Cost Reduction: While the initial investment in robotics systems can be significant, they can lead to long-term cost savings. Robots can optimize production processes, reduce waste, minimize rework, and lower operating expenses by increasing efficiency and reducing labor costs.

Increased Flexibility and Adaptability: Robots can be programmed and reconfigured to perform different tasks and adapt to changing production needs. They can handle a wide variety of products and perform different operations, allowing for quick and seamless transitions between tasks and reducing the need for manual retooling or reconfiguration.

Data Collection and Analysis: Robots equipped with sensors can collect valuable data about their operations and the surrounding environment. This data can be utilized for process optimization, predictive maintenance, and decision-making. Analytics and machine learning techniques can extract insights from the collected data, enabling continuous improvement and optimization.

Assistance and Support: Robots can assist humans in various domains, including healthcare, rehabilitation, and elder care. They can provide physical support, perform repetitive tasks, and offer companionship. Robots can aid in enhancing the quality of life, independence, and well-being of individuals who require assistance.

Exploration and Research: Robots are utilized for scientific research and exploration in challenging environments, such as outer space, deep oceans, or hazardous terrains. They can gather data, conduct experiments, and provide insights into areas that are difficult or unsafe for humans to access.

Innovation and Advancement: Robotics drives innovation by pushing the boundaries of technological capabilities. Research and development in robotics lead to advancements in artificial intelligence, machine learning, computer vision, and sensor technologies, which can have a broader impact across various industries.

It's important to note that the benefits of robotics can vary depending on the specific application and implementation. Additionally, the ethical considerations surrounding robotics, such as the impact on employment and the need for responsible deployment, should be carefully addressed.

CHAPTER-16: RELATIONSHIP BETWEEN ROBOTICS AND AI

Robotics and Artificial Intelligence (AI) are closely intertwined and often work together to create intelligent and capable systems. Here is the relationship between robotics and AI:

Robotics as a Subset of AI: Robotics can be considered as a specific application domain of AI. While AI is a broader field that encompasses the study and development of intelligent systems, robotics focuses on the physical embodiment and interaction of these intelligent systems in the real world. Robotics utilizes AI techniques to enable robots to perceive, reason, learn, and act in their environment.

AI Enables Intelligent Behavior in Robots: AI techniques, such as machine learning, computer vision, natural language processing, and planning algorithms, are employed in robotics to enable robots to exhibit intelligent behavior. AI algorithms help robots understand and interpret sensor data, make decisions, learn from experience, and adapt to changing environments.

Perception and Sensing: AI plays a crucial role in the perception capabilities of robots. AI techniques enable robots to process sensor data, such as visual input from cameras, depth information from sensors, or auditory input from microphones. AI algorithms help robots recognize objects, understand speech, detect obstacles, and extract meaningful information from sensory inputs.

Decision-Making and Planning: AI algorithms are utilized in robotics for decision-making and planning tasks. Robots need to reason and make decisions based on the perceived data and the desired goals. AI techniques, such as probabilistic reasoning, optimization, and planning algorithms, enable robots to generate plans, choose actions, and adapt their behavior to achieve their objectives.

Learning and Adaptation: AI techniques, particularly machine learning, are employed to enable robots to learn from data and improve their performance over time. Robots can learn from human demonstrations, trial-and-error exploration, or large datasets to acquire new skills, refine their behavior, and adapt to new situations. Reinforcement learning, deep learning, and imitation learning are commonly used in robotics for learning tasks.

Human-Robot Interaction (HRI): AI plays a vital role in enabling effective interaction and communication between robots and humans. Natural language processing and dialogue systems enable robots to understand and generate human language. Computer vision techniques facilitate human gesture recognition and facial expression analysis. AI algorithms enable robots to interpret and respond to human commands and gestures.

Autonomous Systems: Robotics and AI intersect in the development of autonomous systems. Autonomous robots are capable of perceiving their environment, making decisions, and acting without direct human intervention. AI techniques enable robots to autonomously navigate, plan paths, avoid obstacles, and make decisions based on the current context.

In summary, robotics and AI are closely connected fields, with AI providing the algorithms, techniques, and tools necessary to make robots intelligent, perceive the world, reason, learn, and interact with humans and their environment. Robotics, in turn, provides the physical embodiment and platform for applying and integrating AI techniques in real-world applications.

CHAPTER-17: HOW TO IMPLEMENT ROBOTICS AND AI?

Implementing robotics and AI involves a series of steps and considerations. Here is a general roadmap to guide you through the implementation process:

Identify the Problem or Task: Determine the problem or task you want to solve or automate using robotics and AI. Clearly define the objectives, requirements, and constraints of the system you aim to develop.

Research and Familiarize Yourself with Existing Solutions: Explore existing robotics and AI solutions that are relevant to your problem or task. Study research papers, publications, and real-world implementations to gain insights and learn from the experiences of others.

Determine the Scope and Resources: Define the scope of your implementation project. Assess the resources you have available, including budget, technical expertise, and infrastructure requirements. Consider whether you will build the system from scratch, use pre-existing platforms, or collaborate with external partners or vendors.

Design the System Architecture: Develop a system architecture that outlines the components, interfaces, and interactions of your robotics and AI system. Determine the hardware and software requirements, sensor configurations, actuation mechanisms, and communication protocols.

Select the Robotics Platform: Choose a suitable robotics platform that aligns with your requirements. Consider factors such as mobility, dexterity, payload capacity, and the availability of software development kits (SDKs) and APIs. Examples of popular robotics platforms include ROS (Robot Operating System) and various robot-specific platforms.

Develop the AI Algorithms: Determine the AI algorithms and techniques that are most suitable for your application. This could include machine learning, computer vision, natural language processing, planning, or a combination of these. Design and train AI models using appropriate datasets, or leverage pre-trained models and customize them for your specific task.

Integrate Hardware and Software: Connect the robotics hardware (sensors, actuators, motors) with the software components. Implement the necessary software interfaces and drivers to enable communication and control between the AI algorithms and the robotic system.

Implement Perception and Control: Develop the perception capabilities of the robot by integrating computer vision, sensor fusion, and data processing techniques. Implement control algorithms to enable the robot to interact with its environment, perform tasks, and execute actions based on AI decisions.

Test and Validate: Conduct thorough testing and validation of your robotics and AI system. Evaluate its performance against the defined objectives and requirements. Test the system in various scenarios and real-world conditions to ensure its reliability, safety, and accuracy.

Iterate and Improve: Collect feedback from users and stakeholders and iterate on your system to address any issues or limitations. Continuously improve and optimize the performance of your robotics and AI system based on user feedback and real-world data.

Deployment and Maintenance: Deploy the system in its intended environment and monitor its performance. Regularly maintain and update the system to ensure its functionality, security, and compatibility with evolving technologies.

Remember, implementing robotics and AI can be a complex and multidisciplinary process. It often requires expertise in robotics, AI algorithms, software development, and integration. Collaboration between domain experts, engineers, and data scientists is often necessary to successfully implement robotics and AI solutions.

CHAPTER-18: HOW TO ASSEMBLE ROBOTS AND AI?

Assembling robots and implementing AI involves a combination of hardware and software components. Here are the general steps involved in assembling robots and integrating AI:

Define the Robot Design: Determine the design and specifications of the robot based on the desired functionality and task requirements. Consider factors such as size, mobility, degrees of freedom, and payload capacity. Choose the appropriate components, such as actuators (motors), sensors, power supply, and communication modules.

Acquire Robot Components: Source the necessary hardware components for your robot design. This may include motors, microcontrollers, sensors (e.g., cameras, proximity sensors, IMUs), chassis or mechanical parts, wheels or legs, and any other specific components required for your robot's functionality.

Mechanical Assembly: Begin assembling the mechanical structure of the robot. Follow the design guidelines or instructions for attaching the components, mounting the motors, sensors, and other mechanical parts. Ensure that the robot is stable, balanced, and structurally sound.

Electrical Wiring: Connect the electrical components of the robot, such as motors, sensors, and microcontrollers, using appropriate wiring and connectors. Pay attention to proper power supply, voltage levels, and signal connections. Follow any provided schematics or wiring diagrams to ensure correct connections.

Sensor Integration: Integrate the sensors into the robot's framework. This involves mounting and connecting the sensors to the appropriate ports or interfaces on the microcontroller or main control board. Ensure that the sensors are correctly calibrated and their data can be reliably acquired by the control system.

Microcontroller/Control System Integration: Connect the microcontroller or main control board to the necessary components of the robot, including the sensors, actuators, and communication modules. Install any required firmware or software on the microcontroller to enable control and communication.

Software Development: Develop or implement the software components required for controlling the robot and implementing AI algorithms. This may involve writing code for the microcontroller, implementing AI algorithms for perception, decision-making, and control, and creating user interfaces or APIs for interacting with the robot.

AI Integration: Integrate the AI components into the software system. This involves incorporating machine learning models, computer vision algorithms, natural language processing, or other AI techniques, depending on the specific application. Train or fine-tune the AI models using appropriate datasets to suit the robot's functionality.

Testing and Debugging: Test the robot's hardware and software components to ensure proper functioning and interaction. Validate the control system, sensor readings, and AI algorithms by performing tests and simulations. Debug any issues or errors that arise and iterate on the design or implementation as needed.

Calibration and Optimization: Calibrate the robot's sensors, actuators, and control system to ensure accurate readings and precise control. Optimize the robot's performance by fine-tuning parameters, adjusting algorithms, or implementing feedback control mechanisms.

User Interface and Interactions: Develop or configure the user interface and interaction mechanisms for controlling or communicating with the robot. This may involve creating a graphical user interface (GUI), voice command recognition, or other methods of interaction depending on the intended user experience.

Deployment and Maintenance: Deploy the assembled robot and AI system in the intended environment or application. Regularly maintain and update the software components, perform hardware checks, and address any issues or improvements based on user feedback and real-world usage.

It's important to note that the specific steps and requirements may vary depending on the complexity of the robot and the AI techniques being implemented. It is recommended to refer to the documentation and resources provided by the manufacturers of the robot components and AI libraries/frameworks for detailed instructions and guidance during the assembly and integration process.

www.ingramcontent.com/pod-product-compliance
Lightning Source LLC
LaVergne TN
LVHW051612050326
832903LV00033B/4469